# Brain

## Injury, Illness and Health

## Steve Parker

Heinemann Library
Chicago, Illinois

Customer Service  888-454-2279

Visit our website at www.heinemannlibrary.com

Design: Jo Hinton-Malivoire and AMR
Illustrations: Art Construction

Originated by Blenheim Colour Ltd
Printed in China by Wing King Tong

07 06 05 04 03
10 9 8 7 6 5 4 3 2 1

**Library of Congress Cataloging-in-Publication Data**
Parker, Steve.
    Brain / Steve Parker.
        p. cm. -- (Body focus : injury, illness and health)
Includes bibliographical references and index.
Contents: Introducing the brain -- Main brain parts -- Blood for the brain -- Brain and head injury -- The brain's building blocks -- How brain cells 'talk'-- The brainstem -- The body's monitor -- Emotions and the body clock -- The sleeping brain -- Cerebellum and movement -- The brain's nerves -- The cerebral cortex -- Two sides of the brain -- At the center of the brain -- Brain infections -- Brain disorders -- Brain development -- The brain in the future.
    ISBN: 1-4034-0748-7 (HC), ISBN 1-4034-3296-1 (Pbk.)
    1. Brain--Juvenile literature.  2. Neurophysiology--Juvenile literature.  3. Brain--Diseases--Juvenile literature. [1. Brain.] I. Title. II. Series: Body focus.
    QP376.P347 2003
    612.8'2--dc21

                                    2002152948

**Acknowledgments**
The author and publisher are grateful to the following for permission to reproduce copyright material:
p. 4 Getty Images/Whit Preston; p. 5 SPL; p. 7 SPL/Scott Camazine; p. 9 Getty Images/Steve Dunwell;  p. 10 SPL/CNRI; p. 12 Getty Images; SPL/Alfred Pasieka; pp. 13, 15, 19, 27, 33 Actionplus; p. 22 Corbis/Michael Cole; p. 24 Alamy Images; p. 28 John Walmsley; p. 31 Getty Images/Ellie Bernager;. p. 32 SPL/Montreal Neuro Institute/McGill University; p. 35 Popperfoto/Reuters; p. 36 SPL/Sinclair Stammers; p. 37 SPL/Dr P. Marazzi; p. 38 SPL/BSIP VEW; p. 39 SPL/GCA/CNRI; p. 40 SPL/Petit Format/Nestle; p. 41 Corbis; p. 42 SPL/Simon Fraser; p. 43 SPL/James King-Holmes.

Cover photograph of a false-color MRI scan of a brain is reproduced courtesy of Science Photo Library/Scott Camazine.

The author and publisher would like to thank David Wright and Kelley Staley for their assistance with the preparation of this book.

Some words are shown in bold, **like this.** You can find out what they mean by looking in the glossary.

# CONTENTS

The human body is made up of many different parts, including the liver, kidneys, stomach, intestines, brain, bones, muscles, and heart. Each part works independently, but all the parts work together in a coordinated manner so that the body as a whole can function and be healthy. The main system specialized for the control and coordination of all body parts is the nervous system. Its most important part is the brain. The brain receives information from outside the body, from the eyes, ears, and other sense organs. It also decides which movements and actions you make and controls the muscles you use to carry these out.

## Brain and mind

The brain is the site of the human mind. It is where you think, have ideas, feel emotions, change moods, express desires, solve problems, and store and recall memories. These are known as higher **mental** processes. You are aware of them in your mind.

There are also many other processes that the brain carries out, which you are not usually aware of. Examples of these include the heartbeat, breathing, and digestion. These are known as lower-level processes. You do not have to think about making them happen. They are part of the automatic brain.

The brain is where you think, understand, store knowledge, and carry out other mental processes.

## Brain trouble

The brain is so complicated and so vital as the body's control center that problems affecting it can have far-reaching effects. Some of these problems have a physical cause, which can be detected and described. This makes them easier to understand. For example, a blow to the head can cause a person to be knocked out to or lose **consciousness,** as the brain is suddenly shaken and bruised inside the skull.

Other brain problems seem to have no obvious cause or reason. An example is the condition of epilepsy. A person with epilepsy experiences a kind of electrical storm in the brain, which can bring on a seizure. Lack of a clear cause may make these brain conditions more difficult to understand, yet they can have far-reaching effects on a person's life.

The medical study of the brain, spinal cord, and nerves, and the disorders that affect them, is known as neurology. The study of the mind and how humans think and behave is known as psychology.

## More knowledge

Brain scientists often say that they have learned more about the brain in the past ten years than in all the years and centuries before. This increasing amount of knowledge continues, week by week, year by year. It is now helping to unravel some of the brain's great secrets, such as how memories form and the puzzle of consciousness.

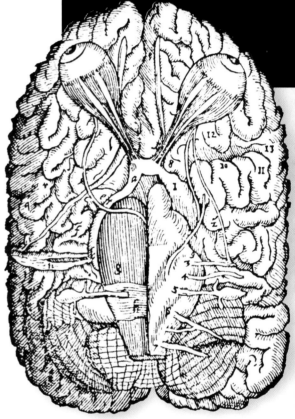

Old diagrams of the brain look strange and outdated today. Will today's diagrams seem strange and outdated in the future?

---

### Main parts of the nervous system

The body's nervous system has three main parts:

- The central nervous system, CNS, consists of the brain and spinal cord.
- The **peripheral** nervous system, PNS, includes the network of nerves that carry messages between various parts of the body and the brain and spinal cord.
- The **autonomic** nervous system, ANS, has parts in both the CNS and PNS. It deals with autonomic, or automatic, body processes, such as digestion and the heartbeat.

The average adult human brain weighs about 3 pounds (1.4 kilograms). It is pinkish-gray, feels like stiff jelly, and is covered with deep, wrinkle-like grooves. The brain has four major parts: the **cerebrum**, cerebellum, diencephalon, and brain stem.

## The cerebrum

The cerebrum makes up about seven-eighths of the brain. It is the large, wrinkled lump that curves over and covers most of the other parts. The cerebrum is the main site of **consciousness**, ideas, feelings, and memories. Some say it is the thinking part of the brain.

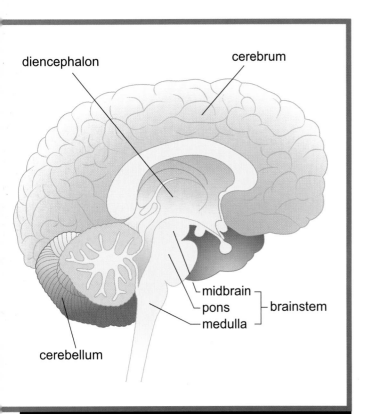

The brain fills the top half of the head. Its lower rear parts extend down to the level of the mouth. It is protected inside the strong, dome-shaped skull bone.

The cerebrum has two parts, or halves, known as the left and right cerebral hemispheres. They are separated by a deep groove. Each hemisphere has an outer, gray, wrinkled layer called the cerebral **cortex.** The two hemispheres are joined by a long strip, the corpus callosum, which carries nerve signals between them.

## The cerebellum

At the lower rear of the brain is the cerebellum, which means "little brain." It resembles a smaller version of the cerebrum, with its rounded, wrinkled surface. Its main task is to deal with nerve signals sent to the muscles. It helps the body keep its balance and posture and to make movements that are smooth, precise, and coordinated, rather than jerky and clumsy.

## The diencephalon

The diencephalon is in the center of the brain, with the cerebrum above and the cerebellum behind. It includes the thalamus in the middle and the **hypothalamus** to the lower front. The diencephalon helps alter your level of awareness, whether you are fully alert, daydreaming, drowsy, or even asleep. It also checks information coming from the eyes and other sense organs—except for the nose—and is involved in moods, emotions, and basic feelings, such as hunger, thirst, fear, and rage.

## The brain stem

The brain stem is the lowest part of the brain. At its base, it tapers downward and passes through a hole in the bottom of the skull. It then merges with the spinal cord, which is the body's main nerve.

The brain stem is the main automatic part of the brain. It deals with essential processes such as heartbeat, breathing, and digestion, which you do not have to think about.

## The energy-hungry brain

The brain looks still and unchanging. However, it is very busy at the microscopic level of body chemicals and electrical signals. Every second, billions of nerve messages flash around inside it. This activity needs energy. The brain forms about one-fiftieth of the body's total weight yet uses more than one-tenth of the body's total energy.

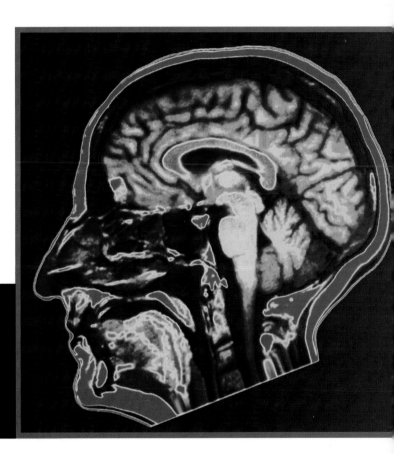

Modern medical scanners can show the living brain inside the head and even pinpoint which parts are working most, by the amounts of energy they are using.

### Keep up the thinking energy

The brain's need for a constant supply of energy can affect the way you think and concentrate. The body's energy comes from food. If you miss a meal, this can reduce the energy supply. You may feel light-headed and unable to think clearly or to make quick, sensible decisions. In sports and other physical activities, it is important to maintain a supply of energy, not only to the muscles, heart, and lungs, but also to the brain.

# AROUND THE BRAIN

The brain is well protected by the hard, domed skull bones. It does not press up against the inside of the skull, but is separated by three sheetlike layers, or **membranes,** with fluid between. These layers are called the **meninges.** They wrap around the whole brain and also extend downward around the spinal cord.

## Fluid around the brain

There is a slight gap between the middle and inner meninges. This is called the subarachnoid space, and it contains a special liquid known as cerebrospinal fluid, or CSF. The liquid forms a pool in which the brain floats, cushioned from blows and vibrations. CSF also fills the subarachnoid space around the spinal cord.

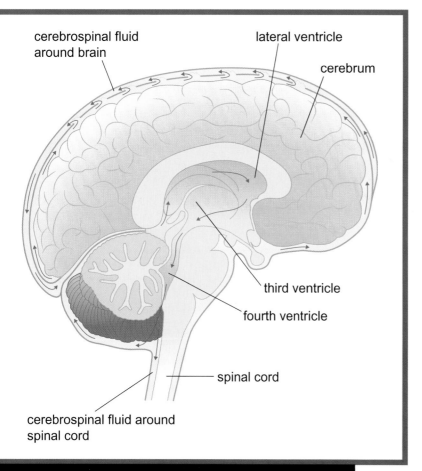

cerebrospinal fluid around brain

lateral ventricle

cerebrum

third ventricle

fourth ventricle

spinal cord

cerebrospinal fluid around spinal cord

The brain is partly hollow, as it contains four chambers known as ventricles. The ventricles are filled with cerebrospinal fluid, which is made by parts of the ventricle lining. It flows slowly through small gaps and openings and out and around the brain and spinal cord.

## Ventricles

CSF is present not only around the brain but also inside it. There are four small chambers, or **ventricles,** inside the brain, linked by passageways. Two are called lateral ventricles, one in each cerebral hemisphere. The third ventricle is in the diencephalon, and the fourth is inside the brain stem.

## Circulation of CSF

CSF is not still. It is made continuously by the linings of the ventricle chambers. It oozes in a slow, one-way flow out of three small passageways from the fourth ventricle and into the subarachnoid space around the brain and spinal cord. It then seeps slowly through the meninges and is carried away by the blood. In this way, CSF collects and removes unwanted substances and wastes from around the brain.

## A sample of brain fluid

In some health problems, a small sample of CSF is taken for medical tests. It is usually withdrawn from the lower spinal cord with a long, hollow needle. This procedure is called lumbar puncture. Presence of blood in the fluid may indicate bleeding, or a **hemorrhage**, around the brain, while certain germs can suggest an infection such as meningitis.

### Added protection

The brain is perhaps the best-protected part of the body. It is surrounded by the layers and fluid of the meninges and by the strong skull bones. Muscle, skin, and hair also protect the head, and some people wear a hat or a helmet. Even so, a blow to the head can cause great damage. Blows or knocks to the head are a risk in many sports and activities, from football to skiing and skateboarding. This is why helmets and other protective headgear are so important, and in many cases, required. A broken arm usually mends; a damaged brain may not.

Hard hats or helmets are required by law at many hazardous sites, including construction and industrial yards.

# BLOOD FOR THE BRAIN

Most body parts have a simple blood supply. Blood arrives along a tube or **blood vessel** called an artery and is taken away along another vessel called a vein. The brain is different. It has four arteries that transport blood from the heart, through the neck, and into the skull. Two of these—the carotid arteries—carry blood mainly to the upper and front parts of the brain. The other two—the vertebral arteries—carry blood to the lower and rear parts of the brain.

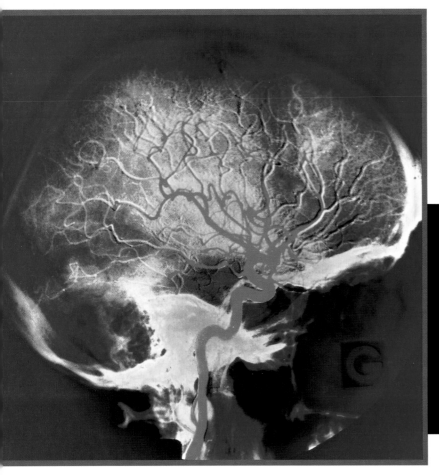

A cerebral angiogram or arteriogram is a specialized X ray that shows the many branching blood vessels that supply the brain tissues with blood. Blockage of a vessel can cause the disorder known as stroke.

## A circular route

At the base of the brain, the four arteries are quite close to each other. They are joined or linked by extra arteries that form a circular route under the brain. This is known as the cerebral arterial circle, or circle of Willis. It is a kind of fail-safe design and ensures that if one artery is blocked or damaged, the others will carry the blood to the parts of the brain it would normally supply.

## The brain's veins

As blood leaves the brain, it does not flow straight into a vein. It oozes into pools called dural sinuses around the top of the brain. These come together at the lower rear of the brain and feed into two main veins, which carry blood out of the skull, back down through the neck, and to the heart.

## When blood supply fails

The brain suffers from lack of blood faster than any other body part. The supply may fail for several reasons, including underlying blood vessel problems, such as narrowing and hardening of the arteries, or a blood clot that travels from elsewhere in the body.

Depending on the part of the brain that lacks blood, symptoms may include weakness, dizziness, headache, numbness, tingling, **paralysis** that affects speech and movement, and loss of **consciousness.**

If a blockage soon breaks up, and blood flow is restored, these symptoms fade. This condition is known as transient ischemic attack, or TIA. (Ischemia is a lack of oxygen being brought by the blood to a body part.) If the blood supply continues to fail, the result is a stroke (see box at right). The symptoms and effects last longer in stroke, and some may be permanent.

### Strokes

In many industrialized countries, strokes cause up to one third of all deaths and long-term disability. There are several reasons for this, including smoking tobacco and eating an unhealthy diet. Both of these habits cause arteries to become narrowed and stiff, increasing the risk of a blood clot. Lack of exercise, being overweight, and high blood pressure can also increase the risk of stroke. However, rapid medical treatment with clot-busting drugs, or perhaps surgery, can reduce many of the immediate problems and also reduce the aftereffects.

A stroke can make it difficult for a person to walk or talk. But many forms of treatment and rehabilitation help a person to return to normal life.

# BRAIN AND HEAD INJURIES

Despite the brain's various layers of protection, it can be damaged by a hard knock or crushing blow. There are several types of damage, which have different effects, and various problems can take different lengths of time to develop. This is why it is important to seek expert medical advice for any kind of hard knock, jolt, or blow to the head or neck.

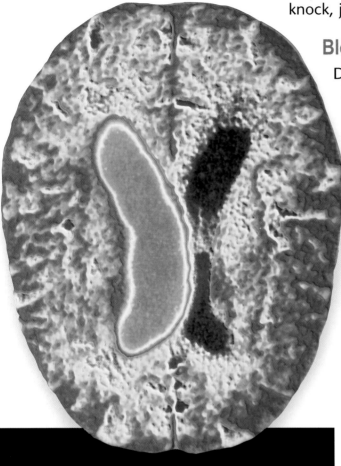

A pool of blood, or hematoma, may collect at the site of a stroke, where blood vessels are damaged and leaking. This presses on the surrounding parts of the brain.

## Blow to the brain

During a blow to the head, the brain may suffer a physical knock, especially on its surface, or **cortex**, as it slams against the inside of the skull. This upsets the millions of delicate nerve messages and can cause minor bruising.

Sometimes, the effects of a blow to the head are limited. For example, a knock on the lower rear of the skull may affect the visual cortex, or vision center, which lies just under the skull. The vision center deals with nerve messages from the eyes. The effect of the blow may be blurred or disturbed vision, and the affected person may imagine seeing stars.

## Concussion

A blow to the head may cause a person to lose **consciousness.** When this happens, the person is said to have been knocked out, have passed out, or have blacked out. This can happen for a few seconds, or perhaps a minute or two. The person then recovers consciousness and comes around or comes to. This temporary, limited loss of consciousness is called **concussion**. It may be followed by a period of feeling dazed, perhaps with memory loss, headache, muscle weakness, and numbness or tingling.

## Bleeding

Another type of damage caused by a head injury is a leakage of blood, known as a **hemorrhage,** from a **blood vessel.** Blood seeping into the brain itself is called a cerebral hemorrhage. If outer vessels rupture, blood may leak around or between the **meninges** layers. This is loosely called a brain hemorrhage, even though the blood is not actually in the brain.

Blood leaks may result not only from head injury but also from other conditions. One is an **aneurysm,** which is a weak region of an artery wall. This can balloon outward and eventually split or rupture.

## Pressure on the brain

In any of these cases, the leak may form a pool of blood known as a hematoma. The hematoma cannot expand outward because of the rigid skull bone. So it presses inward, on the brain. The effects of this pressure include drowsiness, headache, confusion, nausea, numbness, weakness, **paralysis,** and perhaps, long-term unconsciousness or coma.

### Expert attention

Sometimes the effects of a brain injury appear within seconds or minutes, then quickly clear. In other cases, the effects are delayed and only appear slowly, over days or even weeks, by which time the original injury may be forgotten. This is why any injury or hard blow to the head should always receive medical attention as soon as possible after the event.

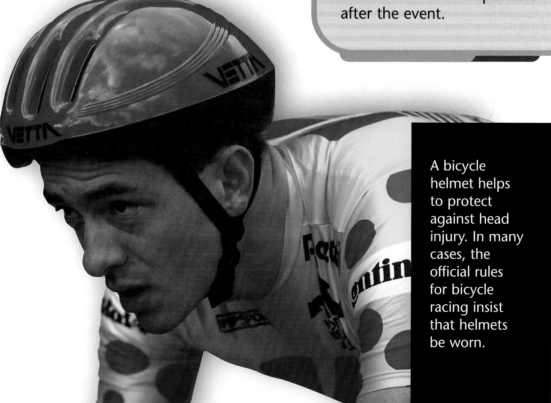

A bicycle helmet helps to protect against head injury. In many cases, the official rules for bicycle racing insist that helmets be worn.

# THE BRAIN'S BUILDING BLOCKS

The brain, like other parts of the body, is made up of billions of microscopic building blocks known as **cells.** The main cells in the brain are nerve cells, or neurons. There are more than 100,000 million of them. They are among the most long-lived and specialized cells in the whole body.

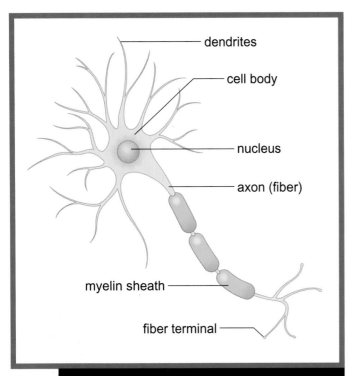

- dendrites
- cell body
- nucleus
- axon (fiber)
- myelin sheath
- fiber terminal

Long extensions called dendrites and an even longer, thicker extension called the axon spread from the main part, or body, of a nerve cell.

## Features of a nerve cell

A typical nerve cell has three main parts:

- The **cell body** is much the same as that of other cells.
- **Dendrites** are long, thin branches that grow from the cell body. They extend outward and branch again and again, becoming thinner each time, similar to a tree's branches and twigs. Dendrites receive nerve messages from other nerve cells and convey them toward the nerve cell body.
- The **axon,** or nerve fiber, is a long, wirelike extension of the cell body. It may have its own fingerlike branches at its end. The main task of the axon is to carry nerve signals away from the nerve cell body and pass them to other nerve cells.

## Nerve cell types

There are many designs of nerve cells in the brain. Some have very short or branching axons. Some have just a few dendrites, while others have thousands. Some have a cell body halfway along the axon, rather than near one end.

Also, some axons are myelinated. This means they have a covering or sheath made of the fatty substance **myelin** wrapped around them. The sheath protects the axon and prevents its messages from leaking away. It also allows messages to travel fast, at 328 feet (100 meters) per second or more. Other axons are unmyelinated and carry nerve messages more slowly, typically at a speed of 3.3 to 6.6 feet (1 to 2 meters) per second.

## Nerve signals

A single nerve signal is a tiny, brief pulse of electricity. It is created by the movement of dissolved **mineral** substances called **ions.** Ions have electrical charges. They are either positive or negative. Sodium (Na+) and potassium (K+) are examples of ions.

Nerve signals do not pass inside the nerve cell but along its outer layer, the cell **membrane.** The membrane has tiny structures in it called ion pumps and channels. They are specialized to pass certain ions through the membrane, which normally acts as a barrier to them.

## The nerve impulse

A resting part of the cell membrane, when no signal is passing, has more sodium ions outside around the cell than it has inside. And it has more potassium ions inside than outside. As a nerve signal arrives, sodium pumps in the membrane pass sodium ions from outside to inside. Then potassium pumps do the same to the potassium ions, but in the reverse direction. These movements of ions cause a spike of electricity, known as the action potential, nerve impulse, or wave of depolarization. This is the nerve signal.

Individual people make a wave through a large crowd— just as particles called ions pass a nerve signal along an axon.

# SIGNALS AROUND THE BRAIN

As you move, see, listen, speak, and think, millions of nerve signals come into the brain, pass around its various parts, and pass out again. The signals travel very fast, at a rate of many feet every second, through billions of individual nerve **cells.**

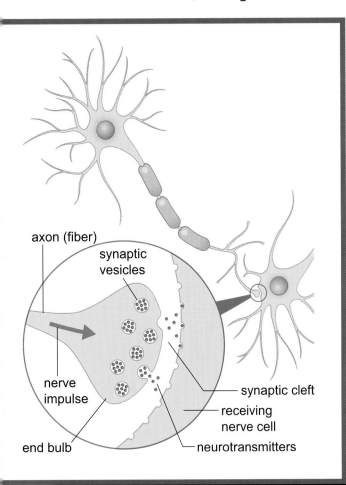

axon (fiber)

synaptic vesicles

nerve impulse

end bulb

synaptic cleft

receiving nerve cell

neurotransmitters

A tiny gap, the synaptic cleft, separates two nerve cells at a synapse. The circle shows an enlarged view with neurotransmitters passing across the gap.

Yet nerve cells do not actually touch each other. Where their **dendrites** and **axons** come together, they are separated by tiny gaps called **synapses.** Nerve signals pass across these gaps by batches of specialized body chemicals known as **neurotransmitters.**

## A gap in the way

At the nerve synapse the **membranes** of two nerve cells are separated by a gap called the synaptic cleft. As an electrical nerve impulse reaches the synapse, it causes the release of tiny amounts of neurotransmitters. These flow across the gap and land on the membrane of the receiving nerve cell, where they fit into specialized sites, called **receptors.** The neurotransmitters change the membrane in such a way that the original wave of electricity from the sending nerve cell begins again in the receiving nerve cell.

## Yes and no

A single nerve signal jumps from one nerve cell to the next, as described above. However, the nervous system is much more complicated. Sometimes, the receiving nerve cell does not fire its own nerve signal until it has received several nerve impulses, one right after another, from sending nerve cells.

Also, some nerve signals from a sending nerve cell cause impulses in a receiving nerve cell, as described, but others reduce the response of the receiving nerve cell, so no signals are sent. In addition, many nerve cells have not just a few synapses, but thousands, linked to many different nerve cells.

The timing of nerve signals also affects how they are received and sent on. The nerve cells also form new synapses with other nerve cells and lose old synapses. Nerve cells create new pathways or circuits for nerve signals around the system. This is similar to what would happen if a computer could continually rewire itself, according to its experiences and what has happened!

## Patterns of signals

The possible pathways for nerve messages around the brain are endless. They also change every day, week, month, and year. This is a central feature of the brain, as shown on later pages. Your awareness, thoughts, decisions, feelings, intentions, ideas, learning, and memories are all patterns of nerve signals passing around the nerve cells of the brain, and they change constantly.

People talk to different individuals at different times. Nerve cells are similar, passing information by way of numerous and changing links called synapses.

### Jumping the gap
The synapse between two nerve cells is about one-hundredth of the width of a human hair. It takes about one-thousandth of a second for neurotransmitter chemicals to pass across this tiny gap.

# THE BRAIN STEM

The brain stem is a highway for **axons** carrying messages between other parts of the brain and the spinal cord. It is also the body's automatic pilot. It houses many control centers for body activities that usually happen in an automatic or **involuntary** way. That is, we do not have to think about them. These centers are part of the reticular formation, which is a series of long, slim bundles of nerve **cells** and their axons lying in the center of the brain stem.

The brain stem has three main parts: the **medulla** oblongata, the pons, and the midbrain.

## Medulla oblongata

The stalk for the whole brain is called the medulla oblongata. It tapers into the spinal cord beneath it. It is about 1.2 inches (3 centimeters) tall and wide. It contains several important control centers:

- The cardiac center regulates the heartbeat.
- The respiratory center controls breathing.
- The vasomotor center regulates the width of **blood vessels** and affects blood pressure.
- The medulla oblongata also contains control centers for sneezing, coughing, swallowing, and vomiting.

## Pons

The egg-shaped pons, or bridge, is chiefly a bypass for nerve signals. It also contains two centers that work with the respiratory center in the medulla oblongata to control breathing.

## Midbrain

The midbrain is not actually in the middle of the whole brain but just below. Like the pons, it contains control centers. Some of these coordinate the way the eyes focus to see clearly and also how they move or swivel in their sockets as the head turns to watch a fast-moving object, such as a racing car. Other control centers pass nerve messages from the ears, about hearing, to the upper parts of the brain.

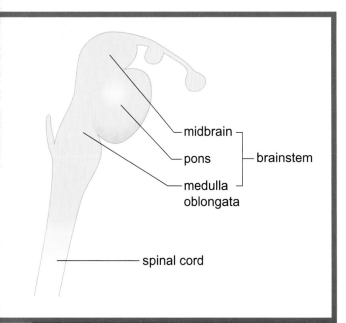

midbrain ┐
pons      ├ brainstem
medulla ┘
oblongata

spinal cord

The brain stem consists of several parts in the lowest regions of the brain. (The upper and rear parts, cerebrum and cerebellum, are not shown here.)

On either side of the uppermost midbrain is a rounded, dark-colored part called the substantia nigra. It is involved in the condition known as Parkinson's disease (see page 35).

## Crossover

Many axons pass through the brain stem, linking body parts and the spinal cord to the upper parts of the brain. In the medulla oblongata, these bundles cross over from one side to the other, forming an X shape.

The crossover structure means that the left side of the brain receives signals from and sends signals to the right side of the body, and vice versa. So, each side of the brain deals with sensations from and controls the muscles in the opposite side of the body.

### Brain stem death
The brain stem is essential for life. It contains centers that control vital processes, such as breathing and the heartbeat. For this reason, doctors check this part of the brain when a person has suffered a severe head injury or a very serious illness. Sometimes, a stopped heart or still lungs can be started again by emergency medical treatment. If the brain stem is not active, however, there is almost no hope of recovery. This is called brain stem inactivity, or brain death.

When people watch fast-moving scenes, such as a sports match or car race, the midbrain helps to control the way the head and eyes move to follow the action.

# THE BODY'S MONITOR

The **hypothalamus** is at the lower front of the brain, roughly midway between both eyes and both ears. It is small, forming less than one–two hundredths of the brain's total size. It contains many important control centers for vital body processes and affects many kinds of behavior, including moods and emotions, and basic desires of thirst, hunger, and sleep.

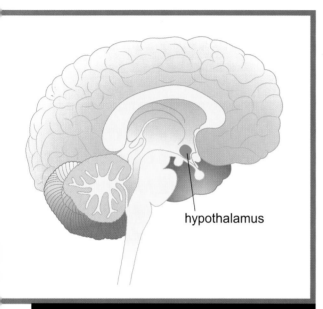
hypothalamus

The hypothalamus is about the size of a grape. Yet it is a major monitoring and control center in the brain.

## Monitoring the body

The hypothalamus contains specialized **cells** that act as sensors to check conditions inside the body. These conditions include the levels of substances in the blood, such as **minerals,** fluids, energy-rich sugars, oxygen, and waste carbon dioxide.

If conditions vary from normal, the hypothalamus sends out nerve messages to other parts of the brain and to body parts to bring the conditions back to normal again. This is part of the overall body process known as **homeostasis.** Homeostasis keeps internal conditions fairly constant, within a narrow range, so that all body parts can work effectively.

## Homeostasis

As an example of homeostasis, the hypothalamus contains thirst centers that check the amount of water in the blood. If the water level falls, these centers make the body aware that it needs to take in extra fluids. The centers also help the body to save water by telling the kidneys to lose less water through urine. Similarly, hunger centers in the hypothalamus control the desire to eat.

## Links with the automatic nervous system

The hypothalamus uses two other body systems as its servants. One is the **autonomic** nervous system. It carries nerve messages from the hypothalamus to the heart, lungs, digestive system, kidneys, skin, and many other parts. These activities are **involuntary.** They automatically keep the body running smoothly.

## Links with the hormonal system

A stalk from the hypothalamus connects it to a small hormonal **gland** called the **pituitary**, which is situated below. The pituitary is the major gland of the whole hormonal, or endocrine, system. It controls many glands around the body and is controlled by the hypothalamus. In this way, the two systems—nervous and hormonal—work closely together to regulate body functions.

## Too cold

Temperature sensors in the hypothalamus control body temperature. If the temperature falls below a certain level, the hypothalamus sends nerve messages to **blood vessels** near the skin, making them narrower. In this way, less heat is lost from the warm blood through the skin. It also tells sweat glands to release less sweat, muscles to twitch (shivering), and body cells to work faster and burn more high-energy sugars. All these processes help make the body warmer. If the body gets too hot, the reverse happens (see box at right). In this way, body temperature is kept within a very narrow range, usually within one to two degrees Fahrenheit (one degree Celsius) from the normal temperature of 98.6˚F (37˚C).

## When the body overheats

In some conditions, such as when exercising on a warm day, the body gets too hot. The hypothalamus detects this and reverses the warming process described at left. It is important to take a break and allow the body to cool itself naturally in this way. Cool water sprays can help, as can staying in the shade and exposing the skin to a fan or breeze.

Feeling too hot and in need of something cool to eat is the result of the hypothalamus at work. It can detect rising body temperatures by amounts smaller than one–one hundredth of a degree. It begins automatic cooling processes and also causes the brain to alter the body's behavior to bring down the temperature.

# EMOTIONS AND THE BODY CLOCK

The **hypothalamus** is not simply the controller of automatic body processes. It is also involved in the behaviors you show during strong emotions and moods.

## Danger!

Do you remember how you felt the last time you faced danger or worry? Your body reacted with signs of fearful behavior. These usually include a faster heartbeat and breathing, tensed muscles, dry mouth, sweaty skin, wide-open eyes, feelings of "butterflies" inside your stomach, and for some people, crying and shouting.

## From thoughts to actions

These reactions are brought about by the hypothalamus, using its links with the **autonomic** nervous and hormonal systems. They prepare the body for quick response and physical action. The hypothalamus only starts these reactions after it receives messages from the thinking part of the brain, the **cortex**. Once the reactions begin, it is very difficult to

stop them by **conscious** thought. They are carried out through the autonomic nervous system, and they progress automatically.

Similar reactions occur with other powerful emotions, such as anger, rage, pain, and great pleasure. They are controlled by the hypothalamus but in response to instructions from the cortex.

Once great panic or rage begins, it is difficult to control. The body's automatic nervous and hormonal processes take over for a time from the conscious, thinking mind.

## The body clock

The hypothalamus contains the body clock, which is a small group of nerve **cells** called the suprachiasmatic nucleus. It is so named because it is just above the optic chiasma, a crossover junction (chiasma) of nerves that carry signals from the eyes to the brain.

Body clock cells have a natural, built-in cycle of activity of about 24 hours. They send nerve signals to many parts of the brain to control a vast array of **biorhythms.** These include body temperature, **hormone** levels, urine formation, digestive activity, injury repair, alertness, and of course, wakefulness and sleep.

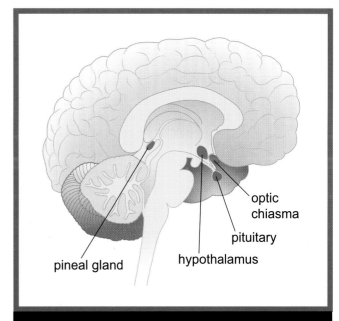

optic chiasma

pituitary

hypothalamus

pineal gland

The body clock is in the lower front of the hypothalamus, just above the optic chiasma, the crossover of nerves from the eyes.

## Adjusting the clock

The body clock receives signals from the optic nerves just below it, bringing information from the eyes about levels of daylight and darkness. The signals continually adjust the clock so that it runs to an accurate 24-hour rhythm. In this way, the body's natural rhythms of alertness, rest, wakefulness, and sleep stay in step with the days and nights of the outside world.

Tests on people who stay in constant daylight or darkness show that the body clock still works. The people in these studies wake up, eat, are active, rest, and sleep in the usual daily cycle. Without changing light levels to adjust the body clock, it tends to run slightly slower, with a cycle of about 25 hours.

## Pineal gland

The pineal **gland,** or pineal body, just above the thalamus, has close links with the hypothalamus and especially with the body clock. It has a role similar to the hypothalamus's and links brain activity to the hormonal system. In particular, it makes and releases melatonin, which is the sleep hormone, under instructions from the body clock.

# THE SLEEPING BRAIN

The brain's **hypothalamus,** body clock, and pineal **gland** control many natural rhythms or daily cycles of activity in the body. Perhaps the most obvious **biorhythm** is the wake-sleep cycle. As you go to sleep, your muscles relax and your heartbeat and breathing slow. The brain, however, stays very busy, as shown by recordings of brain waves, which are obtained using an electroencephalograph (**EEG**) machine.

As you fall asleep, brain waves become longer and lower. This is called slow-wave, orthodox, or deep sleep. It is difficult to rouse a person in this sleep. Sometimes, the person is said to be "dead to the world"!

## REM sleep and dreams

After 50 to 70 minutes of deep sleep, the brain waves become faster, taller, and more irregular. Also, breathing and heart rate quicken and muscles twitch. The eyes move rapidly back and forth under closed eyelids. This stage is **REM** (rapid eye movement) **sleep,** also called paradoxical or shallow sleep.

After 15 to 30 minutes of REM sleep, the brain sinks into deeper sleep again. These periods of deep sleep and REM sleep alternate every 90 to 100 minutes. After a total sleep time of about 7 to 8 hours, the average adult wakes up.

People woken during REM sleep usually report that they have been dreaming. In fact, most people probably dream each night during REM sleep. You actually recall the dreams only if you wake up during or just after the REM period.

The sleeping body seems still and inactive. But vital actions such as breathing and the heartbeat still take place, under the control of the brain, which is also very busy with other processes. However, much of what the brain does during sleep remains a mystery.

## Why do we sleep and dream?

There have been many ideas about why humans sleep and dream. One is that people are sight-based beings who cannot see to move around when it is dark. Therefore, sleeping when it is dark helps people avoid danger, as the body rests and repairs itself. Another idea is that dreams are a random activity of nerve **cells** in the brain, with little meaning. Alternatively, dreams could be a time when the brain sorts out recent thoughts and memories and throws out information that is not important. Dreams could even be a time when the brain works through emotional problems and conflicts.

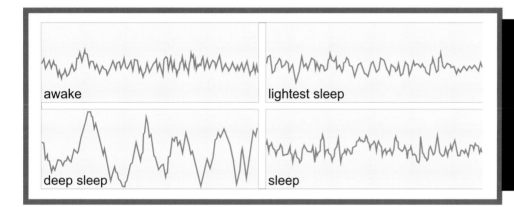

awake

lightest sleep

deep sleep

sleep

Recordings by an EEG machine show many different types of electrical activity in the brain during sleep.

Recent research suggests that dreams are important to forming memories, especially long-term memories. Brain activity during REM sleep involves parts of the brain used in forming memories.

### Disturbed sleep
The body's natural wake-sleep rhythm can be disturbed by very late nights, sudden early mornings, exercise at odd times, shift work, travel across time zones, erratic mealtimes, and stressful events. Symptoms include lack of energy, bad moods, and difficulty sleeping even though the person feels very tired. These are seen in conditions such as jet lag and seasonal affective disorder (SAD), or winter blues, which may result from lack of daylight during long, dark winters.

### Sleeping pills
Various medications work as sleeping pills to reduce brain activity and bring on feelings of tiredness and sleep. Most of these drugs work by interfering with **neurotransmitters** such as serotonin, acetylcholine, **epinephrine**, and norepinephrine. However, some of these drugs can cause dependency and other problems.

You do not have to concentrate on every tiny action you make. You decide to write your name, or tie your shoelaces, or ride your bicycle, and then you find yourself doing so, almost without thinking. Making complicated, skilled movements involves part of the brain called the cerebellum.

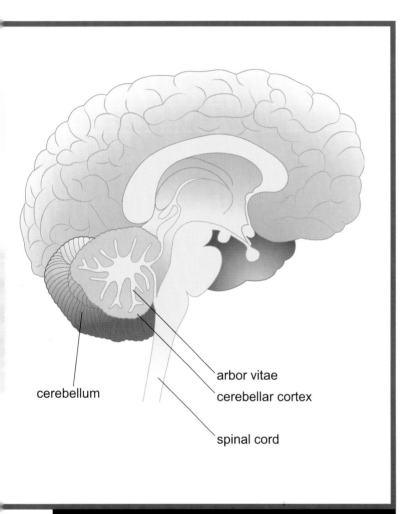

cerebellum

arbor vitae
cerebellar cortex

spinal cord

The cerebellum is the rear lowermost part of the brain. It sits at the back of the brain stem. It has a complicated branching pattern inside called the arbor vitae or "living tree."

The cerebellum is tucked under the rear of the **cerebrum** and has a similar wrinkled, folded appearance. It makes up about one-tenth of the brain's total volume. It has millions of nerve connections, especially with the large domed cerebrum above and the **medulla** and spinal cord in front and below.

## Posture and balance

You can stand up straight, walk, lean, bend, and jog with almost no **conscious** thought. Parts of the cerebellum control these actions. They respond to information coming into the brain from the ears (including the balance sensors), the eyes, and the stretch sensors in the muscles and joints. Together, these messages tell the brain about the position and movements of various body parts, especially the head, neck, and trunk.

The cerebellum sorts through the messages and sends out instructions to muscles, again mainly in the head, neck, and trunk. The muscles work in a precise way to keep the body moving smoothly in a well-balanced manner, so you do not stumble or fall.

## Skilled movements

Two parts of the cerebellum, called lateral **lobes,** one on each side, help to control skilled, precise movements of the arms and hands, legs, and feet. These actions do not start here, however. The decision to move a body part comes from a higher part of the brain called the **motor cortex.** When it arrives as nerve messages at the cerebellum, the cerebellum fills in the details. It sends out thousands of precise complex nerve messages to dozens of muscles, so they pull with exactly the right strength and timing to make the whole movement smooth and coordinated.

The cerebellum also checks movements as they happen and fine-tunes them with small adjustments. Only if a drastic problem occurs does the cerebellum send signals back to the cortex so that your thoughts will turn to dealing with the problem.

A skilled snowboarder uses tiny adjustments to make a fast run down the slope. The main body movements for speed and balance are carried out, almost in an automatic way, by the cerebellum.

### Little brain
*Cerebellum* means "little brain," and the cerebellum looks like a smaller version of the whole brain. It has two domed hemispheres, each with a wrinkled, gray surface called the cortex. The cortex contains mainly nerve **cell bodies** and **dendrites.** Beneath are white masses of **axons** that lead to other parts of the brain.

# THE BRAIN'S NERVES

Often, a computer is hot-wired directly to its most important devices, such as the mouse, keyboard, and monitor. It does not receive or send signals to these parts through a general network. The **cranial** nerves hot-wire the brain. They branch directly from the brain in twelve pairs. There is a left and right nerve in each pair, linking the brain directly to body parts, mostly in the head.

Cranial nerves are known both by their names and numbers, 1 through 12 (or Roman numerals I through XII). Pairs 1 and 2 join to the **cerebrum.** The others join to the brain stem. Some cranial nerves are **sensory.** They carry information to the brain. Others are **motor.** They carry messages away from the brain and to muscles and **glands.** Some are sensory and motor. These are known as mixed nerves.

## Brain and body

Cranial nerve 10, called the vagus nerve, is the largest of the cranial nerves and has the most connections. It branches down to the heart, lungs, stomach, intestines, liver, and kidneys. Various parts of the brain, especially the **hypothalamus** and **medulla** oblongata, receive and send signals along this nerve. It is part of the **autonomic**, or automatic, monitoring and control of body processes.

Speaking involves several cranial nerves, especially 11 and 12 (see chart on page 29), which control the larynx, or voice box, and tongue.

## Facial palsy

Palsy is muscle weakness, or **paralysis.** Facial palsy, also called Bell's palsy, affects cranial nerve 7 (facial), which becomes swollen and pinched where it passes through and along the skull bone. The cause is not clear, although the problem can be set off by a cold wind on the face. The effects are weakness and drooping of one side of the face, with the inability to close the eye, smile, or make facial expressions. Taste may also be affected. The condition usually clears up in a few weeks, perhaps aided by medication.

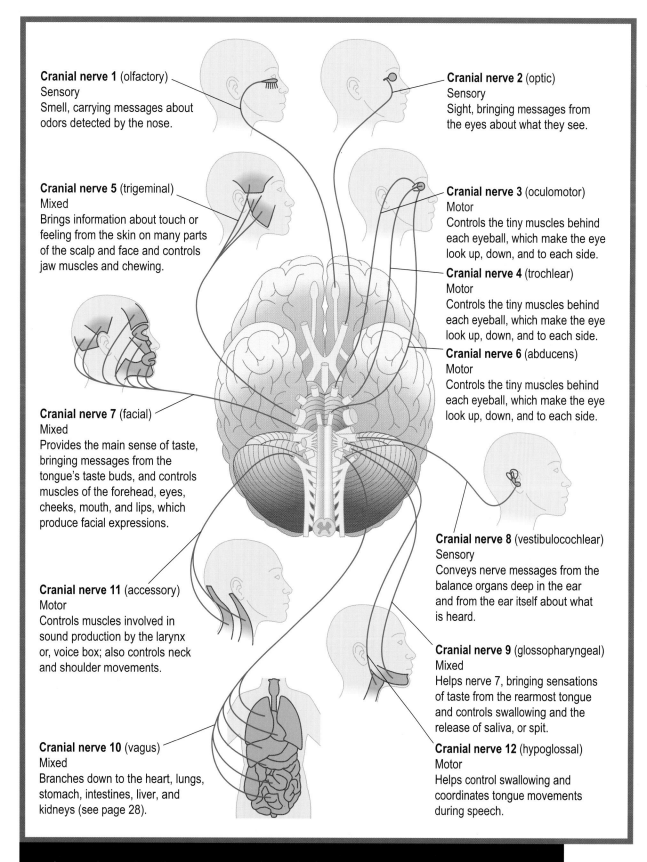

**Cranial nerve 1** (olfactory)
Sensory
Smell, carrying messages about odors detected by the nose.

**Cranial nerve 2** (optic)
Sensory
Sight, bringing messages from the eyes about what they see.

**Cranial nerve 5** (trigeminal)
Mixed
Brings information about touch or feeling from the skin on many parts of the scalp and face and controls jaw muscles and chewing.

**Cranial nerve 3** (oculomotor)
Motor
Controls the tiny muscles behind each eyeball, which make the eye look up, down, and to each side.

**Cranial nerve 4** (trochlear)
Motor
Controls the tiny muscles behind each eyeball, which make the eye look up, down, and to each side.

**Cranial nerve 6** (abducens)
Motor
Controls the tiny muscles behind each eyeball, which make the eye look up, down, and to each side.

**Cranial nerve 7** (facial)
Mixed
Provides the main sense of taste, bringing messages from the tongue's taste buds, and controls muscles of the forehead, eyes, cheeks, mouth, and lips, which produce facial expressions.

**Cranial nerve 8** (vestibulocochlear)
Sensory
Conveys nerve messages from the balance organs deep in the ear and from the ear itself about what is heard.

**Cranial nerve 11** (accessory)
Motor
Controls muscles involved in sound production by the larynx or, voice box; also controls neck and shoulder movements.

**Cranial nerve 9** (glossopharyngeal)
Mixed
Helps nerve 7, bringing sensations of taste from the rearmost tongue and controls swallowing and the release of saliva, or spit.

**Cranial nerve 10** (vagus)
Mixed
Branches down to the heart, lungs, stomach, intestines, liver, and kidneys (see page 28).

**Cranial nerve 12** (hypoglossal)
Motor
Helps control swallowing and coordinates tongue movements during speech.

The twelve pairs of cranial nerves branch directly from the brain's underside, mainly out to parts of the face, head, and neck. Cranial nerve 10 runs down through the neck to parts in the chest and lower body.

# THE CEREBRAL CORTEX

The outer layer of the brain's main part, the **cerebrum**, is called the cerebral **cortex**. It is about one-tenth of an inch (3 millimeters) thick, gray in color, and folded into bulges and grooves, which increase its surface area to about the size of a pillowcase. The cortex contains more than 50 billion nerve **cells**, with their **cell bodies** and spiderlike **dendrites** and **axons** passing to the inner brain parts.

## Centers of the cortex

The cortex is the thinking brain. It is the main site for **conscious** thoughts, where you are aware of your surroundings, your actions, and yourself. On each side, it is divided into larger bulges, or **lobes**. In each lobe, different parts called areas, or centers, deal with nerve messages coming in from or going out to certain body parts.

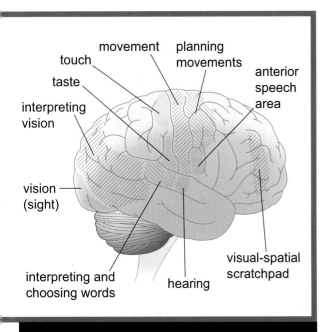

movement · planning movements · touch · taste · anterior speech area · interpreting vision · vision (sight) · interpreting and choosing words · hearing · visual-spatial scratchpad

Areas or patches of the cortex, the outer layer of the cerebrum, deal with different parts of the body and various parts of the thinking or mental processes.

## Frontal lobe

The frontal lobe is under the forehead. The front part of it, sometimes known as the prefrontal lobe, is concerned with expressing excitement and emotional feelings.

On the side of the frontal lobe is the visual-spatial scratch pad. It carries a short-term memory of your surroundings. This is how, after a quick look around a room, you can walk through it with your eyes closed and not bump into objects. You have a mind's eye picture of the room in this part of the brain.

Toward the rear of the frontal lobe is a strip down the side called the **motor** cortex. It oversees muscle control to make body movements. At the rear lower corner is the Broca's, or anterior, speech area, which is involved in speech.

## Parietal lobe

The parietal lobe is at the rear side of the brain. At its front is a strip that runs down the side, called the touch cortex. It receives information from the skin about what you touch and feel. Like the motor cortex just in front, different patches of the touch cortex deal with different body parts—face, head, neck, torso, arm, and so on. The lowest part of this area deals with taste information.

## Temporal lobe

The temporal lobe is under the temple, or above the ear. It contains the **auditory** cortex, which sorts information from the ears about what you hear. It also contains the vestibular cortex, which maintains balance and posture, and part of the Wernicke's, or posterior, speech area.

When you look at a scene intently, the lower rear part of the cortex, known as the visual center, is very active and interpreting what the eyes see.

## Occipital lobe

The occipital lobe, at the lower rear of the brain, is mostly concerned with receiving and sorting nerve messages from the eyes. The visual cortex has several centers that deal with different aspects of vision, such as what the eyes see in various parts of a scene, recognizing items from memory, identifying them, and putting the parts together into a meaningful overall picture. The lobe also contains part of the Wernicke's, or posterior, speech area.

### Forced time-out

In many sports, any head injury that is followed by a blackout, or **concussion**, means that the player must leave the action and have an urgent medical checkup. This is followed by days or possibly weeks of rest. If the brain parts that control movement are not working well, players or athletes are more likely to put themselves in danger with clumsy, awkward movements or slow reactions.

The main part of the brain, the **cerebrum,** is made up of two halves, known as the cerebral hemispheres. As explained earlier, **axons** from one side of the body cross over to the other side in the lower brain. The left cerebral hemisphere deals with nerve signals to and from the right side of the body, and the right hemisphere deals with signals to and from the left side of the body.

A straplike bridge of more than 200 million axons, called the corpus callosum, links the two hemispheres. This allows them to share information and send signals to each other.

## One side takes over

The cerebral hemispheres look similar to one another. In a very young child, they also work in a similar way. Gradually, by the age of five to eight years, one side becomes dominant or in charge. This is usually the left hemisphere, which controls the right side of the body, including the right hand. Most people—about nine out of ten—use mainly their right hand for precise, intricate tasks. Even in most left-handed people, the left hemisphere is dominant.

The left side of the brain usually dominates the right side and controls the right side of the body. So, detailed hand movements for a right-handed person, and the main control of speech, come from the left cerebral hemisphere. The colored areas shown here are associated with speech.

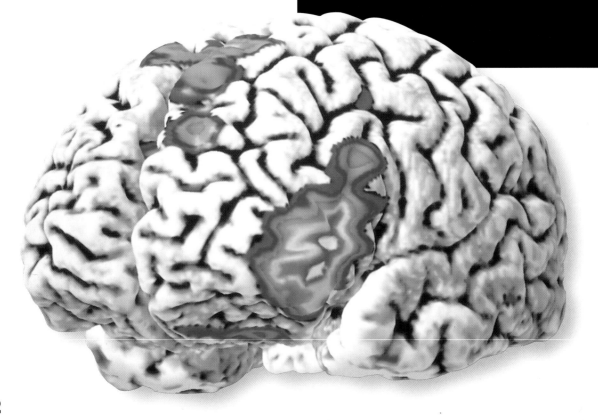

## Speech

Most processes in the brain occur through connections among several parts. Speech is an example. The left, or dominant, posterior speech area recognizes and understands spoken words and selects the words for a reply. The left anterior speech area then organizes the patterns of nerve messages to speak the reply.

## Two halves make the whole

There are general differences in the way in which the two hemispheres of the brain work. The left side is more concerned with language, reason, logic, numbers, and math. It figures out steps and stages and how individual pieces function.

The right hemisphere deals more with general ideas and concepts, overall shapes, colors and forms (such as quickly recognizing a face), art and music awareness, intuition, and jumping to an idea or conclusion.

The left side of the brain tends to pick out details, while the right side sees and understands the whole idea. Both sides work together and help each other.

## Dyslexia

Dyslexia is a group of conditions that affect a child's ability to read, write, spell, and learn. In many cases, the child is otherwise normal, or has above-average **mental** skills. Aspects of dyslexia include reading letters or words backward, such as *b* instead of *d,* or *on* for *no.*

Different forms of dyslexia have different causes. These include **genetic** influences, the way nerves develop in the unborn baby's brain, and the way the eyes and brain work together. Some children with dyslexia have learning difficulties, simply because they cannot read properly. If their dyslexia is identified early and followed by expert tutoring as required, they can learn to read well and progress at speed. Treatment of dyslexia is increasingly successful.

Planning possible moves in a game of reason and logic, such as chess, largely involves the left side of the brain.

Under the the **cortex,** or the thinking part of the brain, lie bundles of **axons** called **white matter.** They carry messages between the cortex and many other parts of the brain. One part is the thalamus. The thalamus monitors the **sensory** information, except for smell, that travels from other brain parts toward the cortex. It checks whether the information is important. For example, as you sleep, your ears hear normal night sounds. If there is a strange sound, the thalamus identifies it, and you awaken. The thalamus is also involved in control of movements, **biorhythms,** and your level of alertness, from fully alert to resting, drowsy, or asleep.

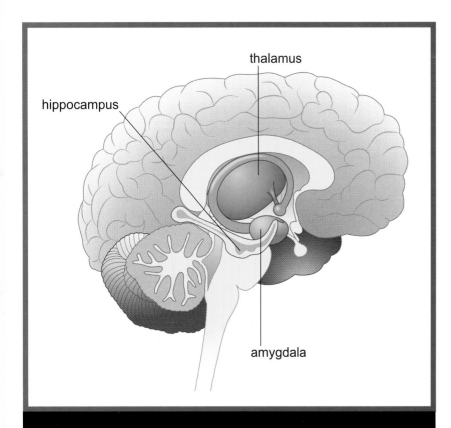

hippocampus

thalamus

amygdala

The middle parts of the brain are involved in a wide variety of mental processes, including conscious thought, precise movements, and memory formation.

## Basal ganglia and limbic system

In the lower center of each cerebral hemisphere are groups of **gray matter** called basal **ganglia.** They have many links with the cortex and the thalamus. They are involved with movement and behavior—any actions that are smooth and purposeful.

The limbic **lobe** is a ring-shaped region on the lower, inward-facing surface of each cerebral hemisphere. It works with other parts of the brain as the limbic system. The limbic system takes part in memory and emotions and the reactions and behaviors they cause. For example, when you recall a frightening event from long ago, and it still makes you feel cold and clammy and your heart race, this is due partly to the limbic system.

The olfactory cortex, or smell center, is a patch on the limbic lobe surface. It deals with nerve messages that come from the nose. Because the olfactory cortex is closely linked to the limbic system, certain smells can cause powerful memories and feelings.

## Parkinson's disease

Parkinson's disease mainly affects parts of the basal ganglia. It is caused by problems with chemicals called **neurotransmitters**. In this condition, the brain cannot control certain movements, especially those people do almost without thinking, such as swinging the arms when walking. The disease causes shaking or trembling, slow or jerky movements, muscle stiffness, and changed posture. A person with the condition tends to walk with a stoop, using short, shuffling steps.

After the age of 60, about 1 person in 200 develops Parkinson's disease. Misused drugs and certain brain infections can produce similar symptoms called Parkinsonism. Medication and other treatments are very helpful to lessen the symptoms, for a time.

In recent years, former world heavyweight boxing champion Muhammad Ali has been affected by Parkinson's disease. The way he has coped with this disabling condition has inspired millions of other people with the disease.

### Memory

There is no single memory center in the brain. Many parts are involved, including the cortex (especially of the frontal lobe), hippocampus, amygdala, and thalamus. The information contained in memories is probably stored as pathways among the billions of interconnected nerve **cells.**

You use your short-term memory to retain facts for seconds or minutes, such as a telephone number you are about to call. By the next day, the memory has gone. The hippocampus helps turn short-term memories into long-term memories. Long-term memories include information you need for weeks, years, or a lifetime, such as your name and where you live.

Certain germs, or harmful **microbes,** can infect the brain. They attack either the brain directly or as part of an infection elsewhere in the body. Infection in the brain itself is quite rare. Many germs travel around the body and reach the brain by way of the blood, but the **blood vessels** in the brain have a special structure in their walls that limits what can pass through. This is called the blood-brain barrier. Unfortunately, the same barrier also limits the ability of medications to pass from the blood into the brain itself.

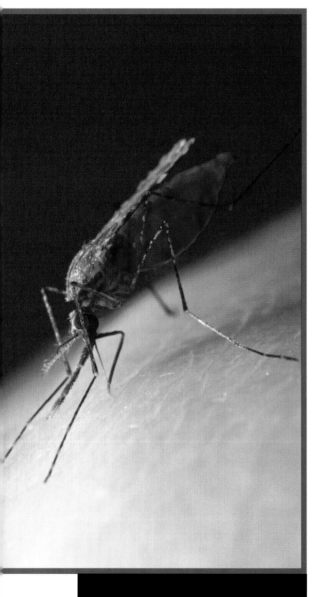

As they take blood, mosquitoes can infect people with cerebral malaria.

Some germs are types of **bacteria,** which can generally be attacked with **antibiotic** drugs. Other germs include **viruses,** which are rarely affected by antibiotics. Viruses can, however, be treated by a growing range of antiviral drugs.

## Encephalitis

Swelling and **inflammation** of the brain is known as encephalitis. It may be caused by a virus that attacks the brain or it may occur as the result of another viral disease, such as mumps or measles.

Mosquitoes and ticks spread some kinds of encephalitis viruses. In tropical regions, tiny single-**celled** parasites can cause the problem. For example, the sleeping sickness parasite is spread by tsetse flies.

Symptoms of encephalitis may be similar to those of any mild illness, such as headache, fever, and tiredness. The symptoms may progress to more serious drowsiness, sensitivity to bright light, loss of muscle power, disturbed speech and sight, and even **unconsciousness.**

With good care and medication, most people recover from encephalitis. However, there is a risk of brain damage or even death for babies, older people, and those with other illnesses.

## Meningitis

In a healthy person, the cerebrospinal fluid around the brain is clear and watery. In some infections, it becomes milky or cloudy. This occurs especially in meningitis, which is swelling, or inflammation, of the **meninges** layers around the brain. The germs may spread from an infection elsewhere, such as the ear, or be part of a general infection, such as tuberculosis or mumps. In some cases, the germs enter through a head wound or injury. Certain viruses that cause meningitis spread through the air and affect a number of people in the same area as a small epidemic.

### Other brain infections

In some cases of the tropical disease malaria, the brain is severely affected. This is known as cerebral malaria, and it may cause symptoms similar to those of a stroke, perhaps with seizures. It requires urgent medical attention.

The condition of AIDS, which is caused by the HIV (human immunodeficiency virus), may affect the brain and cause various symptoms.

## Effects of meningitis

There are many forms of meningitis, both viral and bacterial, and they vary from mild to life-threatening. Symptoms include a dark skin rash, headache, fever, stiff neck, nausea, vomiting, and sensitivity to bright light. Without urgent medical treatment, some patients become drowsy and lose **consciousness.**

The condition is often more dangerous in babies and young children. They cannot describe their symptoms well, and they are at greater risk of brain damage and permanent disability.

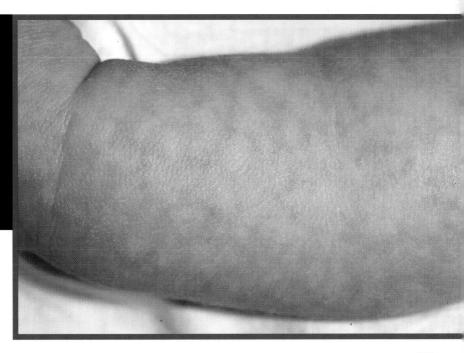

A red or dark skin rash, as though hot and flushed, is one possible symptom of meningitis. Unlike other rashes, the dark color may not become lighter when the area is pressed.

# BRAIN DISORDERS

The brain can feel pain in all parts of the body, except in itself. It does not have suitable pain-sensing nerves. A headache is not usually a brain-ache. It is pain from the **blood vessels**, nerves, or **meninges** around the brain. A headache is not usually a disorder itself but a symptom of another problem. Causes of headache vary hugely, from head injury or food allergy to an infection, brain **tumor**, physical or emotional **stress**, or the effects of drugs such as alcohol.

## Migraine

Severe headaches that tend to come back, often on one side of the head, are known as migraines. There are usually other symptoms before or with the headache, such as nausea or vomiting, disturbed vision, or sensitivity to light and noises. Sometimes, before the migraine, there is a strange feeling or sensation, such as flashing lights or zigzag lines in front of the eyes.

Sensors on the head pick up tiny electrical signals that ripple out from the brain and through the skull and scalp skin. The resulting brain waves are called an electroencephalogram (see box on page 39).

Some migraines are brought on by triggers, which vary from emotional stress or high blood pressure to eating chocolate or drinking alcohol. Migraine can also run in families. In many instances, the pain seems to be caused by a narrowing, then widening, of the blood vessels in or around the brain. Modern medications are very effective at helping most people with migraines.

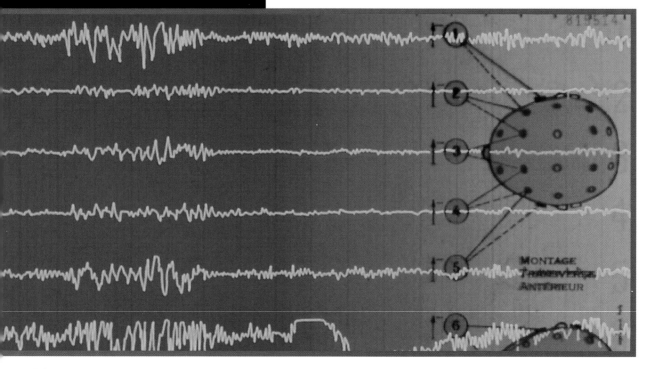

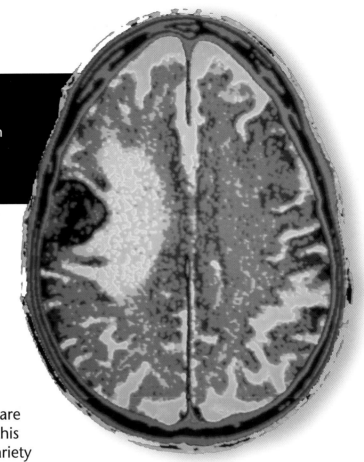

This colored computed tomography scan shows a human brain with brain cancer, the dark patch on the left.

## Seizures and epilepsy

There are many forms of seizures. They vary in intensity from a brief period of faintness, perhaps with strange sensations such as an odd taste in the mouth, to a severe attack, with a blackout and violent, uncontrolled movements called **convulsions.** These types of events are often known as epilepsy, although this is a term used to describe a wide variety of conditions.

Some kinds of epilepsy have a known cause, such as a brain tumor. In other cases, nerve **cells** seem to fire at random as a kind of electrical storm rages in the brain. About 1 person in 130 develops epilepsy. Drugs called anticonvulsants are successful at treating most cases.

## Brain tumors

A growth, or tumor, can occur in the brain, often for no clear reason. It tends to press on the brain and cause various symptoms depending on its location. These vary from headache and nausea or vomiting, to sight problems, loss of balance or sense of smell, seizures, muscle weakness, and even personality changes. Treatment may include an operation, **radiotherapy,** drugs, or all three. Generally, the sooner treatment begins, the higher its success rate.

### Brain waves

Millions of electrical nerve signals pass around the brain every second. Sensor pads placed on the skin of the head can detect these signals. They show up as wavy lines on the screen or paper strip of an electroencephalograph (**EEG**) machine. The size and shape of the brain waves help scientists study what the normal brain does, for example, as a person sleeps. EEG recordings also help doctors identify disorders such as epilepsy and stroke.

# BRAIN DEVELOPMENT

The brain is one of the first body parts to develop. About three weeks after conception, the whole body is slightly smaller than a grain of rice and is shaped like a letter C. At this stage, there is no sign of a head with a brain inside. From the fourth week, the brain grows faster than any other body part. It bulges hugely, becoming almost one-third of the size of the whole tiny body, with the spinal cord as its tail. Nerves begin to grow and branch from it, as the eyes and other parts of the face and head take shape.

About five to six weeks after the body begins to develop, the brain is by far the largest part, bulging above the eye and face.

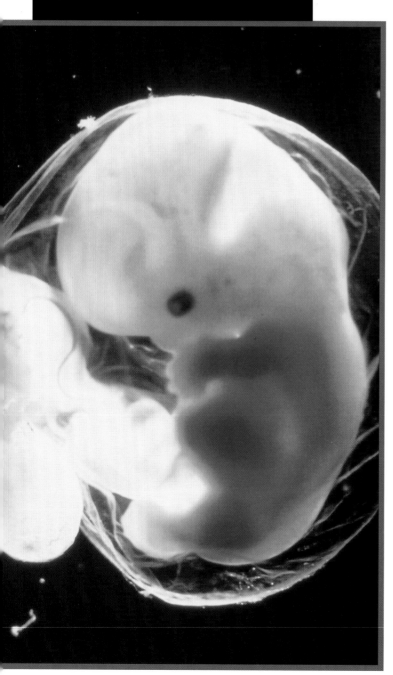

After this early burst of brain growth, other body parts begin to catch up as the baby develops in the womb. By about week twelve, the overall shape of the brain is formed, but the cerebral hemispheres are still smooth. Their first wrinkles or grooves appear over the next few weeks.

## Invisible growth

A new baby's brain weighs less than a pound, slightly less than one-quarter of its adult size. It makes up around one-tenth of the baby's total body weight, compared to one-fiftieth in an adult.

In the first year after birth, the brain weight rockets to about 2.2 pounds (1 kilogram), two-thirds of its final adult size. Its growth then slows during infancy and childhood. This is also the main time for making new links or connections between nerve **cells,** as learning happens at an incredible speed. The brain's final growth spurt is during the teenage years. The brain reaches its full size at 14 to 16 years of age.

Almost every day, a baby or young child learns new physical and mental skills—both based in the brain.

## Sex and the brain

The typical male brain is slightly larger than a female one, because a typical man is larger than an average woman. However, the female brain is bigger, compared to the size of the female body, than the male brain is to the male body.

There are no outer differences between a woman's brain and a man's. Recent research does show that the brains of females and males develop in different ways, even before birth. The differences are partly due to the effects of sex **hormones**, which are natural messenger chemicals made by the sex organs—ovaries in females, testes in males.

Even at birth, the brains of baby girls and baby boys have different wiring diagrams. This allows each to become better at certain thinking tasks as they grow, although environment and upbringing can also have a great effect. Here are some examples of the differences:

- Most women are better than most men at word-based tasks, such as remembering and recalling words from lists.
- Most men are better than most women at shape-based tasks, such as identifying objects seen from different angles.

### Seeing the brain
The brain can be seen or imaged by various types of medical machines and scanners.

- CT (computerized tomography) and MRI (magnetic resonance imaging) scanners show small details of brain structure.
- PET (positron emission tomography) scanners show which parts of the brain are using the most energy. This is similar to showing the parts that are thinking hardest.
- Cerebral arteriogram (angiogram) is a type of **X ray** that reveals the **blood vessels** in the brain and shows if they are narrowed or blocked.

Scientists know a lot about the brain. Yet there is still much more to learn. Research continues around the world, especially into the way that chemicals affect the brain. Some chemicals are recreational drugs that can devastate a person's intelligence and reason. Others are helpful medicines for problems such as migraine, epilepsy, Parkinson's disease, and severe depression.

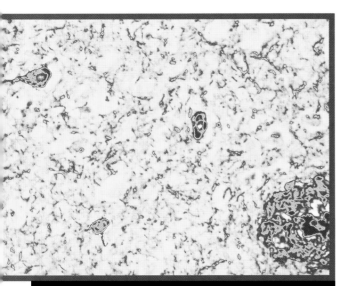

This colored light micrograph shows brain tissue from a person with Alzheimer's disease. The diseased tissue is shown in blue.

## Behavior and psychology

The brain is the site of the mind. The workings of the mind—**mental** activity—are studied by experts such as psychologists and psychiatrists. There are many types and degrees of mental problems. Severe sadness or depression, extreme mood swings in manic depression, schizophrenia, autism, phobias (excessive, unfounded fears), compulsive actions, obsessive desires, and addictive behavior are just a few. Some of these have a physical basis, perhaps caused by a brain **tumor.** Others are chemically based, possibly due to problems with nerve signals jumping from one nerve **cell** to the next. Other problems have no clear cause.

## The aging brain

Nerve cells are very specialized in their shapes and connections. After birth, they rarely multiply to produce new cells. From about the age of twenty years, the brain loses a tiny fraction of its weight each year. This loss may speed up slightly in old age.

The aging brain may have reduced mental powers—or it may not. There is huge variation from person to person. In senile dementia, mental abilities are lost more rapidly than normal, from about the age of 60 or 70 years. There is usually failing memory (especially of recent events), anxiety, and difficulty speaking, expressing thoughts, and making sensible decisions.

In Alzheimer's disease, the changes of dementia occur earlier, perhaps from the age of 30 or 40. The brain itself shows signs of dead or tangled nerve cells. There are also objects, called plaques, around nerve cells that disrupt their signals, and there is a lack of **neurotransmitter** chemicals.

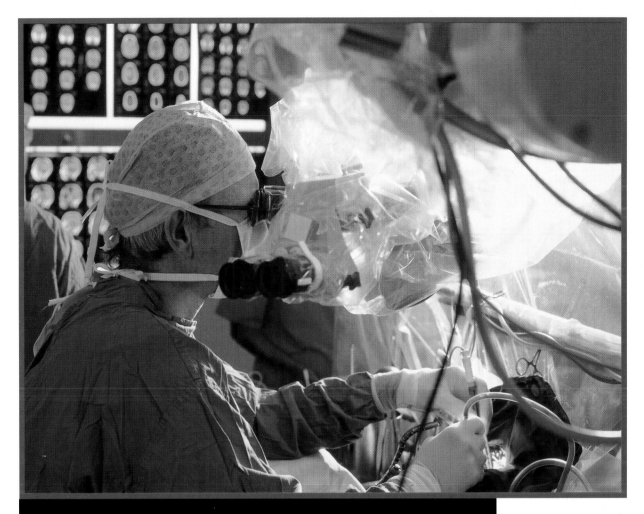

Through an operating microscope, the neurosurgeon can see and manipulate single axons.

## Future treatments

Medical treatments for brain problems improve every year. There are more effective drugs with fewer side effects. Often these are designed with computers. Surgeons can operate on the microscopic level of individual **axons**. Substances called neural growth factors encourage damaged or cut nerve cells to repair or grow again.

Scientists once thought that the adult brain could not make new nerve cells. However, it can, in parts such as the hippocampus and the olfactory, or smell, areas. The new nerve cells are formed by stem cells. There is much research into the use of stem cells as future treatments for disorders such as Parkinson's disease and Alzheimer's disease.

### Are bigger brains smarter?

There is no link between brain size and intelligence. On average, the size of the brains of people regarded as geniuses in their fields—science, philosophy, art, and sports—show no difference from the brain sizes of ordinary people.

# WHAT CAN GO WRONG WITH THE BRAIN?

This book has explained the different parts of the brain, how they work, and how they may be damaged by injury and illness. This page summarizes some of the problems that can affect young people. It also gives information about how each problem is treated.

Many problems can be avoided through simple, practical health measures such as exercising regularly, getting plenty of rest, eating a balanced diet, being careful with high-risk activities, and having a positive attitude. This page shows some of the ways you can prevent injury and illness.

Remember, if you think something is wrong with your body—or your **mental** state—talk to a trained medical professional, such as a doctor or your school nurse. Regular medical checkups are another important part of keeping your body and mind in good health.

| Illness or injury | Cause | Symptoms | Prevention | Treatment |
|---|---|---|---|---|
| meningitis (several forms) | infection by germs (**bacteria** or **viruses**) that spread from elsewhere in the body or through the air or that enter through a head wound or injury | depend on the form, but include headache, fever, stiff neck, nausea, vomiting, fear of bright light, dark skin rash, drowsiness, loss of **consciousness** | take measures to protect against head injury, including wearing seat belts in vehicles and using protective equipment such as helmets in hazardous sports or pursuits | medical assessment, rest, and medications depending on the type of germ |
| brain or head injury | severe physical shock may cause bleeding (**hemorrhage**) in or around the brain or skull fracture | pain, confusion, memory loss, headache, muscle weakness, numbness or tingling, temporary loss of consciousness (**concussion**) or long-term **unconsciousness** | take measures to protect head, including wearing seat belts in vehicles and using protective equipment such as helmets in hazardous sports or pursuits | urgent medical attention, especially after loss of consciousness (however brief), even if the symptoms appear temporary, due to the risk of serious aftereffects |

| Illness or injury | Cause | Symptoms | Prevention | Treatment |
|---|---|---|---|---|
| dyslexia (a group of conditions that affect the ability to read, write, and spell, and so affect general learning) | varied, including **genetic** influences, nerve development in an unborn baby's brain, nerve coordination of eyes and brain | problems with reading and perhaps writing, such as perceiving letters or words backward, for example, *b* instead of *d*, *on* instead of *no* | early recognition is extremely important, or the child may receive unsuitable help with learning | expert tutoring as required to improve reading, writing, and other skills |
| facial (Bell's) palsy | **cranial** nerve 8 (facial nerve) becomes swollen and pinched when it passes through and along the skull bone | weakness and drooping of one side of the face, inability to close the eye, smile, or make facial expressions; taste may be affected | no specific measures | possibly medications, rest, medical monitoring |
| epilepsy (several forms) | may be linked to brain injury, damage, or **tumor,** or high body temperature; many have no clear cause | **convulsions** or seizures that recur, varying from short episodes of apparent daydreaming to random, jerky body movements, loss of muscle control, and **unconsciousness** | recognizing and avoiding triggers in individual cases, such as flickering light, certain emotions, or **stress** | anticonvulsant drugs; mental techniques such as distraction; more rarely surgery |

# 🏃 FURTHER READING

Farndon, John. *The Big Book of the Brain.* Columbus, Ohio: McGraw-Hill, 2000.

Hayhurst, Chris. *The Brain and Spinal Cord.* New York: Rosen, 2001.

Hickman Byrnie, Faith. *101 Questions Your Brain Has Asked about Itself.* Brookfield, Conn.: Millbrook, 1998.

Landau, Elaine. *Head and Brain Injuries.* Berkeley Heights, N.J.: Enslow, 2002.

# GLOSSARY

**aneurysm** weak area or balloon-like swelling in a blood vessel

**antibiotic** type of medical drug that kills bacteria

**auditory** having to do with hearing

**autonomic** able to work on its own or carry out actions by itself

**axon** long, thin part of a nerve cell that carries signals away from a nerve cell body

**bacterium** microbe that can cause infection

**biorhythm** body process or condition that varies in a regular way, day and night

**blood vessel** tube that carries blood around the body

**cell** microscopic unit or building block of a living thing. The body is made of billions of cells.

**cell body** main part of a cell

**cerebrum** main dome-shaped upper part of the brain, consisting of two cerebral hemispheres

**concussion** short-term blackout or loss of consciousness

**conscious** having mental awareness

**consciousness** state of being aware of what is happening and being able to respond

**convulsion** movements, usually jerky and random, caused by uncontrolled contraction of muscles

**cortex** outer layer of a body part such as the brain or kidney

**cranial** having to do with the cranium, the dome-shaped upper skull

**dendrite** thin, branching part of a nerve cell that carries nerve signals toward the nerve cell body

**EEG** electroencephalograph; machine that detects and displays the brain's tiny electrical nerve signals

**epinephrine** neurotransmitter and hormone substance that prepares the body for sudden physical action

**ganglia** lump-like bulge, especially along nerves or in the brain

**genetic** having to do with genes, which are the instructions for life and exist as the genetic material known as DNA

**gland** body part that makes and releases a product (usually a liquid) such as a hormone

**gray matter** part of the nervous system formed mainly of nerve cell bodies

**hemorrhage** leak of blood, bleeding

**homeostasis** keeping conditions inside the body constant and stable

**hormone** natural chemical substance that affects the workings of specific body parts

**hypothalamus** small part of the brain concerned with vital life functions. It has close links to the hormonal system.

**inflammation** swelling, redness, soreness, and perhaps pain

**involuntary** happening without the need for thought or decision, that which cannot be controlled at will

**ion** tiny particle of a substance that is positive or negative

**lobe** rounded part of an organ or body part

**medulla** inner layer of a body part such as the brain or kidney

**membrane** skinlike covering or lining layer

**meninges** three layers or membranes wrapped around the brain and spinal cord

**mental** having to do with thoughts and the mind

**microbe** very small living thing, only visible under a microscope

**mineral** chemical needed by the body in very small amounts. Calcium and iron are minerals.

**motor** having to do with muscles and the movements they make

**myelin** fatty substance wrapped around certain axons

**neurotransmitter** chemical substance that passes a nerve message from one nerve cell to the next, across a gap called the nerve synapse

**paralysis** inability to move

**peripheral** around the edge, away from the middle or center

**pituitary** master hormone gland, just under the front of the brain

**radiotherapy** treatment involving radiation such as X rays

**receptor** place or site that receives or accepts a specific substance, similar to the way a lock receives a key

**REM sleep** rapid eye movement sleep; a type of light or shallow sleep when dreams usually occur

**sensory** having to do with detecting or sensing conditions, substances, or energy, such as the way the eyes sense light rays

**stress** adverse, difficult, or challenging conditions from physical fatigue or lack of food to emotional worry

**synapse** gap between two nerve cells where nerve signals pass

**tumor** lump-like abnormal growth or swelling

**unconsciousness** mental state of not being aware

**ventricle** fluid-filled chamber or cavity in a body part, such as the brain or heart

**virus** very small microbe that can cause infection

**white matter** part of the nervous system formed mainly of axons

**X ray** form of energy, as rays or radiation, that passes through soft body parts such as flesh but is stopped by hard parts such as bone

# INDEX